Broken Circle

CHILDREN OF DIVORCE
AND SEPARATION

Karen Klein

Thank you to the participants of the *Broken Circle* project. I am grateful for your openness and honesty in sharing this very private part of your lives. Your clarity and insight has been the soul of this project. I know you will face your future with as much courage as you have shown in addressing your past.

And a special acknowledgment to my children. I know it was a bumpy road you traveled.

Broken Circle-Children of Divorce and Separation project is not pro or con divorce but an opportunity for this population to share their personal life experiences in a way that may help others.

Copyright ©2013 Karen Klein
Published by Talking Crow

ISBN 978-1492892250

Broken Circle brand and book design:
Michael Lizama | Blue Torpedo

Digital edition 3rd printing 11/2015

Broken Circle—Children of Divorce and Separation

The *Broken Circle* project gives voice to young adults talking about how their parents' divorce or separation impacted their lives-then and now. It offers a powerful, succinct testament as to how young people navigate these complex emotional seas. Given the opportunity, this population has poignant, often painful and illuminating observations to share: personal life experience that may help others. Their written statements moved back and forward in time, each one a revelation of the life-altering events and memories before, during, and after their family breakup.

This is not pro or con divorce, but a vehicle to enlighten and inform people who can most benefit by it-the children, their parents, therapists, counselors, the judicial system and academia-to understand the unintentional consequences of the parents' split.

My interest in children of divorce began with my personal experience. I divorced in 1980, but only with time did I realize my children had been affected in ways I had not anticipated. In 1987 I began to explore this subject photographically, collaborating with college students aged 18 to 24 who came from divorced families. I made black and white portraits of each person and they wrote their response to my questions: "How are you impacted by your parents' divorce? How does it affect your perceptions, plans, goals, hopes, and aspirations regarding relationships, commitments, and thinking about your own future marriage and children?"

In 2011, a friend in the process of divorce inspired me to revisit the subject using the same questions. The result is *Broken Circle-Children of Divorce and Separation*.

Karen Klein, November 2013

Mary

My parents fought a lot when I was younger. I never thought anything of it. To me, it was completely normal. The first time I heard them mention divorce, I cried as loud as I could upstairs so that they would hear me and stop fighting. I was a rather passive-aggressive child. My dad told me not to worry; he said they wouldn't get divorced and that everything would be okay. Looking back on it now, though, I wish they had gotten divorced much sooner. I blamed myself for a long time for keeping them together when they didn't belong that way.

But things continued to get worse. They continued fighting, and more and more I started to withdraw from everyone and everything around me. I felt helpless and alone, because I didn't want to tell anyone— friends or teachers or even my parents— what effect all of this was having on me. I made myself into an emotionless rock. I tried to kill every emotion that came to me. I still hate crying in front of people because I see it as a sign of weakness.

I've spent so long hiding everything I feel and everything I am, and making up lies to make it look like I'm normal, and putting up a front of who I think I should be, that in all honesty, I don't know who the hell I really am. ○

Arturo

The divorce of my parents was a great satisfaction to me, because it meant the end of fights and the beginning of a new stage in my life with a lot of peace. I had to become the man of the house during adolescence and take some responsibilities because my father left our home.

This event has helped a lot with my personal growth, because I became a more independent and secure person. Despite the distant relationship between my brothers and me with my father, it got better because, due to his absence at home, he paid more attention to us.

I learned that a divorce is not something to get traumatized about, but better yet a new opportunity to create wonderful things in your life; when two people don't get along well, it is better to get separated —everyone deserves to be happy.

Anney

I was 5 or 6 years old when my parents divorced. I had sensed tension for a while, so in a sense it was almost a relief when my dad moved out. I had a really hard time adjusting to bouncing between two households. The majority of my time was spent with my mom and I remember always missing my dad a lot.

Now I have major doubts about the possibility of a lasting, happy marriage. If I find the right person I won't let that stop me, but I know it will be hard to get past that. All of my relationships have been filled with anxiety about my partner leaving me or not wanting to be together anymore—especially towards the beginning.

After my parents divorced I never wished for them to get back together because I knew that it simply wouldn't work. Our family was more functional in two households. I think this is what gives me the most anxiety about relationships—after many years, no matter how great those years are, they can fall apart. ◯

Jessica

My parents divorced when I was 18, and, although perhaps unknown to my dad, it was a long time coming. During the divorce proceedings, my father attempted suicide, and the police came and pulled a shotgun out of his mouth. My mother obtained a protection order against my dad, which led to a series of events essentially forcing my sister and I to each choose a parent. I became very estranged from my mother and felt as though she viewed me as my dad. My dad continually bashed my mom to me, and since I was the only one left who would listen, I did. Both my sister and I struggled with depression and an overall feeling of disconnectedness. I felt as though I had no family, that my family didn't care about each other. Why would I want to live in a world where the people in my life who are supposed to love each other the most actually despise each other? My relationship with my sister became stronger and we began to depend on each other for a source of family.

My perceptions and aspirations regarding relationships/marriage/children have no doubt been affected by my parents' divorce. I don't have a whole lot of faith in the institution of marriage, and certainly don't expect my future partners to be faithful. With the mental illness and divorce history in my family, I don't think I could provide a stable home for children. Although I foresee success for myself and am optimistic about what I will accomplish, I do not view myself as a capable parent. Make no mistake, it has taken several years for me to take something positive out of this situation, but because of the divorce and the way it made me feel, I make a concerted effort to build others up, make them feel special, show friends unconditional love, and have a goal of leaving an overall positive impact when I'm gone.

Clara

My sister and I grew up in a family with a single pillar that was my mother; supported always and unconditionally by my maternal grandmother and supported also with the another who became like my grandmother and my mother too—the lady with whom my mother came to work with. The decisions of my parents, good or not, never contemplated setting us aside.

When I am asked if this has affected me, I usually say I doubt it, but I know that it has. I think perhaps it has affected my way of thinking, of not needing a man to do "men's" stuff, and also no fear of raising a child by my own if I don't have a partner, etc.

It is difficult to know whether my life would have been better if my father had been with us during these years, but surely it would have been different. I respect both of my parents, but give special thanks to my mother—for the courage, strength and her unconditional support to motivate us to move forward.

Logan

My parents' divorce sent me some really confusing messages about relationships. I had a hard time accepting that falling in love was a real thing or believing that there was anyone out there who is perfect for me. I have always felt skeptical about getting married because divorce has haunted my perspective of how special that union is supposed to be. People vow to stay together "'til death do us part," but what they mean is, "'til one of us is fed up and files for divorce."

Within the past few years, a special person has come into my life and made me see that my parents' mistakes don't have to determine my future. Hard times have come into my relationships, and my parents' divorce has made them even harder, but it just takes the right person to prove every doubt wrong.

Cassidy

I had a different experience with divorce than many. It happened when I was very young, so I never remembered it. Throughout my childhood and teen years, I was always relieved my parents were not together because hearing them fight over the phone was bad enough. I knew if it was every day in person, it would have been hell.

I think because so much of my generation grew up with divorce, we look at relationships differently. I see marriage as a way of life, a choice, something that requires constant work and adaptation. Marriage is not a temporary situation that has a plan b-divorce. I do not feel like my parents shared that view.

Jessie

My parents separated when I was 12 years old, so I have experienced high school and college with divorced parents. I think the details of my parents' divorce have been the hardest on me. It wasn't mutual, wasn't expected, and the thing that has affected me the most is the amount of lying and deceit that came out of it. I've had a hard time forgiving my parents for the aftermath and how the whole situation turned out.

In each of my relationships I've found trust to be really difficult for no real reason. I've been with people who clearly care about me very much, but for some reason I find it hard to believe that they don't have secrets they are hiding from me. I feel like it is so easy for people to lie and be dishonest and that most guys are so easily tempted. And the worst part is that I do deeply down know that this isn't the case, that it's ridiculous, but sometimes my mind just goes into those places. And it obviously causes lot of problems in my relationships, but I work hard every day to try and regain my trust for others.

I think that I'm in a better place now than I ever have been in both my personal relationships and my relationship with my parents. And I believe I can break this cycle and be in a truly happy and trusting relationship.

Michelle

My parents had a great relationship while they were married. The first 14 years of my life, I had a solid family. When my mom left our family, moved to Colorado, and ended her 22-year marriage with my dad, it was devastating. But, my parents used the communication and problem-solving skills they had previously displayed, to make the divorce as easy as it could be for my brother and me. When I vehemently asserted that I wanted to stay with my dad in Minnesota, they listened to me and I was allowed to stay.

I struggled with the loss of my family, but I also learned that families take different forms. My dad, brother, and I were still a family. I found other communities in which I felt at home: in the families of my closest friends, and the community of teachers and mentors at school. My father provided support and stability and encouraged me to work on my relationship with my mother. My close relationship with my father is one of the most important things in my life and I see it as a positive outcome of my parents' divorce.

My dream of having a legal career became even more important to me after the divorce. Through it all, I have always believed that marriage can work. I believe that someday, I will have a happy family built around a long-lasting marriage.

Omar

My parents separated before I was born, so I was raised with the idea that not living with both parents was something normal and for a long time I didn't recognize the impact that the separation of my parents had on me. I grew up without brothers, just with my mother. The relationship with my father has not been very close. Just recently I started to reflect on the effect that being the son of separated parents has had on me; and contrary to what I thought at the beginning, this situation has influenced a lot in my personality.

One of the influences that the separation of my parents has had on me is the way I relate to other people. I always have given more importance to family and friends, and never paid too much attention to romantic relationships. I now see at this age my friends care to have stable and enduring romantic relationships, however for me this is not a priority and I have never included them in my priorities.

I recognize that living with a partner is an important element in the life of every individual and I hope some day to be able to form a stable family where the possibility of a divorce does not negatively impact the tie that binds us.

Sydney

My parents divorced when I was six months old, so I have never seen my parents living together or raising me together. I think the fact that I have never seen two people maintain a solid relationship has had a bigger impact on my life than I will ever be able to realize or understand.

I am impacted by my parents' divorce in many ways. I am usually the communicator between my parents so I am always involved in every single decision that is made about me. Sometimes I wish my parents would be able to talk to each other and figure things out without having to communicate through me. I wish that I would have been able to see a functioning relationship as I was growing up so I would know what a healthy relationship should be like for me in my future.

My parents' divorce affects my view on relationships quite a bit. I usually view relationships as a waste of time and I often feel like I don't need an emotional or intimate relationship. I often see them as automatically going to fail and therefore, not worth my time. Being a child of divorce has probably had the biggest impact on me—more than any other event in my life—but I have learned so much about what I want and I hope I can develop a life-long relationship, raise healthy and happy kids, and be a good role model for my children in the future.

Teagan and Nyssa (fraternal twins)

T (left): This is definitely a topic we never talk about. I act like it doesn't affect me, and to a point it doesn't except for the little things like when people say I should ask my "parents."

In regard to relationships, I hope to get married and have a happy family and that we stay together, but in trying to find someone I know I have no standards for the guy to live up to, and I'm always afraid to stand up for what I want because I'm afraid they'll say I'm a needy girlfriend and leave. What I've found is that people with both parents have the confidence that if the guy leaves, he's not worth it. But for me, I believe if the guy leaves me I'll never find another one and that I'm the one who's defective—not him. That definitely is the worst part.

I never had a person, on the male side, to tell me how I should be treated and how I'm special and only deserve someone who treats me right. It was a long path trying to learn that all by myself.

N (right): This is a topic for me that does not get brought up often to get to talk about. The splitting of my parents has affected me in more ways than I think I realize. It is harder for me to trust male figures in my life because of my dad leaving. The one man that was supposed to be there for me through thick and thin has never been there. I know in my future I do not want my kids to go through what my two sisters and I had to. ◯

Robin

My parents divorced when I was ten. The divorce itself was definitely necessary. My dad left us to be with his new wife and unborn baby. Being so okay with the divorce itself, I was very unprepared for the sense of abandonment that I felt for the next several years.

I felt embarrassed and ashamed-like I wasn't good enough. It took me a really long time before I stopped taking the situation so personally, and only recently have I begun to be honest about my family situation, even to my closest friends.

My parents' divorce has made me skeptical of whether people can truly stay happily together for their whole lives. I really do hope to experience it, but I'm still waiting to be convinced that it's possible. Having only had a few relationships, and only one really serious one, I am definitely conscious of the fact that I am not quick to trust and I am scared to make myself vulnerable.

Josephyne

When my parents divorced I was very little and wasn't conscious of what was going on. Even though I didn't live through the divorce or go from one home to another, it doesn't mean that I was indifferent to the situations and realities that children of divorce go through.

In the beginning, it is possible that you won't see what the absence of a parent figure implies; you grow up and you get accustomed to that, you can't miss what you have never had. But sometimes, when you are around functional nuclear families—in meetings, graduations, any event that implies the presence of both parents—you acknowledge that those figures are necessary. Children are not asked to be born. The fact that parents are separated doesn't mean that they have to separate themselves from the children. The parenting role doesn't finish with a divorce order, it is for life.

I consider myself an emotionally, socially and psychologically stable person. I know I shouldn't share my life with just anyone. I should look and wait for the correct person and then if it doesn't work, it is better to separate and leave good memories.

Andrew

My mom divorced my biological dad when I was 18 months. I don't remember this. She remarried and her second husband adopted me. He was a very traditional, mid-west raised stoic athlete, with a military background and he and my mom had a daughter. I found it very difficult to get along with him. My mom wanted to go back to work, which became an issue and they fought constantly; that grew in intensity and I remember a huge, intense tear-filled fight they had while I was watching the Salt Lake City Olympics in 2002. They divorced when I was in 5th grade.

My mom married a 3rd time, and my step-dad is very different from my (adopted) dad. He's become quite withdrawn and I see her unhappiness. They don't have big fights, but they have lots of deep issues, discussion, and hurt about his children.

Divorce for me, as bad as it is, has become so removed from the feeling associated with the word. My own relationships have directly suffered from this because I latch so quickly onto someone. I have a huge hope my relationships will be longer, but I'm too scared to let myself think that because of the realistic part of me; divorce is common, the luster of marriage is gone.

Mayumi

My parents' divorce has impacted my life in multiple ways. While people often attach negative connotations to divorce and the repercussions it can have on families, there are a lot of positive outcomes that have evolved in my life because of my parents' separation. In today's society, divorce is becoming increasingly more common, and in some ways it is refreshing. The reality is that people change, relationships do not always last forever, and it is often more detrimental for kids to live in a chaotic home with two adults trying to make a bad marriage work than to just move on.

I truly believe that the divorce has made me a stronger, more flexible, and open-minded person. I am grateful to both of my parents for the impressions they have made on my life, for introducing me to other adults who have cared for and supported me, and for making an effort not to allow their own differences to get in the way of my relationships with them.

LaTia

When my parents divorced, I was 13 years old and my brother was 8. My parents were together for 15 years, and married 11 of those 15 years.

A marriage is a relationship that two people created with each other and a commitment to continue building that relationship. A divorce happens for a myriad of reasons. My parents love us very much, and no matter what happens in their separate lives they will always be there for their children, and is what will tie them together for the rest of their lives.

As for the future, my dreams and goals are becoming a reality now that I'm focused on dance at the University of Minnesota. Marriage is something that can wait. I wouldn't be disappointed if it never happened. I can make myself happy. I will never have any children of my own. I might adopt after I'm retired and done living my life.

Whitney

My parents had been together, though not married, for twenty-three years and told me they were splitting up the weekend I graduated college. It was a time of change and uncertainty for me and I felt as if I was forced to grow up and cross the bridge from childhood to adulthood. I moved all of my things out of the house, became financially independent, and had to demonstrate a great deal of emotional maturity, all in a short period of time.

I became a sort of referee between my parents since they were not married and could not go through the formal divorce process, which put me in a difficult position and resulted in drama and hurt feelings. My father eventually decided that he no longer wanted any contact with me, which hurt the most as we had been very close. This became real for me when my father would not return my calls on Father's Day and did not acknowledge my birthday. My mom has been really supportive, however, which I am grateful for.

As a result of this I know I have put up an emotional wall. My increased independence has come with a cost since is hard for me to trust others and I consider relationships to be very fragile. For now I choose to focus on my professional life and hope that I will heal with time.

Max

My parents were divorced when I was 2 years old. Throughout my life I have lived with my mother. I consider myself a mama's boy. In all of the relationships I have had, I've treated my girlfriends as princesses. If there is anything I have learned from my parents it was that unconditional love can exist outside of a traditional family.

My father was not around often when I was a child, but I have mended the broken relationship, yet still side with my mother on any opinions they differ in. I plan to wait to get married until I am certain that I am going to spend the rest of my life that person. I do not want to put kids through what I went through, even though I consider my childhood fruitful.

I will forever love my mother and respect women because of her, and I will remember that people, like my father, can change.

Sarah

I don't remember my parents being together, nor would I want to imagine it. My father used to pressure me into the weekend visitations. I locked myself in the bathroom on many occasions, throwing fits, not wanting to leave my mother. He would make me feel guilty for not calling him more often.

I remember him saying that my Aunt Nancy never had a healthy relationship with a man because she didn't have one with her father. He told me the same thing would happen to me. My father constantly accused my mother of putting false ideas about him into my head. The truth is, she never spoke ill of him. She wanted me to have a chance to make up my own mind about him, and at every turn, I saw the awful truth she never shared with me.

I was forced into adulthood at a young age and made several attempts to have any relationship with my father. I called it quits at age twelve. My spirit became lighter once I let go of him. I realized that I couldn't make him be the father I needed him to be. I saw him when I was sixteen, on a street corner—he didn't recognize me.

Vivian

I was born in the United States and my parents were married until I was 3 years old. When they separated, my mother brought me to the Dominican Republic, where I was raised. I didn't have problems with my dad because he was always willing to come and see me every year on my birthday, but sometimes it felt strange not to have a paternal figure close to me.

For a few years after the divorce, my parents didn't get along very well. My father had a girlfriend, which made me feel very uncomfortable. I asked myself, "Why does my father prefer to be with other people instead of my mom and me?" I started to understand that sometimes relationships don't work, and that is normal.

I do think that it taught me to analyze and reflect a lot before committing to one person. If I have children within a marriage and things don't work out, I hope to handle the situation as my parents have because it is a good example that relationships can have a good ending, and not everything is necessarily ugly.

Erin

My parents were married for 18 years before they decided to split up. It happened at such a crucial part of my life when I was transitioning into a teenager. I was very emotional and angry with them for not being able to make it work. I was embarrassed to tell my friends because I grew up in such an affluent area where divorce did not occur very often. I lived with my mom, as my dad moved to Texas soon after. It was very hard for me to be that far away from him since I had grown up with him around all of the time.

I was able to finally accept what had happened by talking to school counselors, peers, and my friends. Going through middle school and high school, my mom was my number one supporter and really gave up a lot for my brother and me. All in all, we grew very close and it was a normal upbringing for us.

While this wasn't an ideal event in my life, it definitely made me stronger and independent. My brother and I made a promise to each other that we would be in relationships much different from our parents'. We know the importance of communication and love in relationships, and our promise is a reminder to each of us that we can create a different future. ○

Ricardo

The separation of my parents affected me a lot. I thought that could never happen to me and I didn't understand how some of my friends could live without their parents together. When it happened, I was 13 years old and had had the best summer of my life, until the last day of vacation—my father was no longer at home. I cried, I called him, asked him, and never had clear answers until several years later.

Despite this, I've always been very optimistic and look for the good things in everything. So in this way I decided to be happy. I took the opportunity to share more with my parents in separate ways. My mom loves the beach and to go out in the city, and whenever I can I go with her to enjoy those things. However my dad loves riding horses, the mountains, being away from the city, so my dad and I spend weekends doing what he likes.

Having separated parents has helped me to be independent, see different points of view. I would have liked to have a close-knit family but I prefer that if they are going to be fighting or angry, it is better for them to have their separate lives and be happy, because seeing them happy makes me feel very good. I am always in contact with them and they support me in everything.

Emily

Divorce is something I have never really talked about with anyone. I realized that I'm not okay with this and I am really hurt, betrayed, and heartbroken.

The day I found out my father was lying to me, the day he told me what he had done to my mother, all the nights he came home late, the nights he didn't come home at all because he was sleeping with her—something inside of me shut off.

I never understood why kids that had divorced parents were so upset and hurt. Now I know why. I've forgiven, but I'll never forget.

Naomi

My parents divorced when I was around 6 years old. I remember them arguing in the night, while I was hiding behind a chair. Although I heard them argue, I never really understood what was going on. A few months later, I saw how my mother packed my father's clothes in a suitcase. It was at that time my mother explained to me that she wanted a separation.

I can say that my parents' divorce didn't affect me too much emotionally, but it did impact my relationship with my father, whom I saw infrequently during the first years of the divorce. Fortunately, in the last few years we have rescued our relationship and now we speak every week.

My mother is my rock, my model to follow, who inspires me to reach my goals and supports me in all my decisions. I live in a very stable home and I find myself very happy. I believe in marriage, but I also consider that divorce is necessary when marriage doesn't work anymore.

Megan

I had some initial bad feelings about the divorce. Obviously because everything in the media portrayed this awful, dramatic event and scary changes that were out of my control. That was true—changes did happen but I'd never known my parents as a happy couple. My image of "love" had never and never will be my parents. So in that sense, I seek the idea of perfect love from role model characters (my mentors, etc.).

I guess the divorce gave me more hope for women and how strong they can be. I always aim to be as strong as my mother in life and relationships of all kinds. Seeing her go through such traumatic events really gave me comfort in knowing that even if I can't control a situation or relationship, I can control my self and what I make of things. ◯

Kira

My parents divorced when I was in fourth grade and I was completely blindsided by it. My sister and I had always known that my Dad would go through phases of what we called being "half-awake, half-asleep", but in truth his drinking problem was the impetus for my mother to end their marriage. I remember reading a book about a girl close to my age whose parents were divorced and being delighted with the idea of double the toys and double the birthday presents! This was not the case and I learned very quickly just how angry my father was at my mother by enduring countless rants where he would slander every possible aspect of my mom.

While I wish I could take away the pain my parents divorce made for everyone involved, I am also grateful for the insight and foresight it has brought me. I matured at a much higher rate than my peers and mastered how to stick up for myself and (more importantly) the ones I love. I have found my determination and maturity to be among the strongest parts of my personality.

As far as marriage goes for me, I find it to be a very dire quest. I grow anxious sometimes at the weight of having to choose the right "one" to marry on the first try, because I do not want to become a statistic. ◯

Josh

My parents divorced when I was very young. I have a few memories of us as a three-person family, but those are heavily outweighed by the years of living with my mom and weekend visits with my dad.

Divorce showed me reality. Every child dreams of having the perfect family, but that ideal never comes to fruition; I had the perfect model in my mind, but lived the actual situation. It was a hard thing for me to accept that the perfect family I so desperately yearned for would never come to reality.

Nevertheless, though it was a very hard circumstance, it has molded me into a young adult with (hopefully) a better grasp of what happens in life. I have led my life with a firmer sense of mindfulness—this is who I am. And in the end, that is possibly one of the most invaluable things I could ever achieve for myself.

Becca

My parents met in third grade, started dating in high school, and got married at 18. They were married for twenty years and got divorced when I was four. I really am lucky because I don't remember the pre- and post-divorce fighting. They've been getting along for as long as I can remember now. I live with my mom, but my dad still comes over almost every day.

Yet despite how well my parents get along post-divorce, there were still side effects. Divorce isn't something people understand or talk about, despite how common it is today. I still get weird looks when people find out my parents are divorced. It has also instilled in me that I should never count on a man. My mom had so much strength throughout my life and has done everything on her own. It taught me to be independent and not rely on anyone.

But that also brings up problems in relationships of my own. I've never been in a serious relationship because I don't want to end up counting on someone and them letting me down—I guess I am just scared. The biggest difference I see in my outlook on love and my friends whose parents are still together is that they still see the "happily ever after" in marriage. Whereas I expect that I'll get divorced someday, and I want to be ready for when that day comes. The reality is that no matter how pleasant or horrific the divorce, it leaves a mark on the kids.

Ana

My parent's divorce made me happy. My whole childhood they stayed together until both my brother and I were in college, in order to maintain a family unit for us children. There was always so much tension and bitterness in the house. My parents are both incredible individuals but had a hard time dealing with things on the same page. When they finally split they both had a new energy for life, which I am so grateful for. They still communicate with each other and we can reunite, on occasion, as a whole family, on good terms, and enjoy the time we spend together.

My fiance also came from a broken home so we have talked about the importance of creating a positive, healthy and happy home for our family in the future. We have both observed our parents battle divorce for different reasons and have negative feelings about some things that we went through as children that we shouldn't have been exposed to. We understand the severity of the decisions we will make as parents, and we will take our vows of working as a unit very seriously because of what we have both experienced.

Mass-Vianet

My parents divorced before I was born. I don't remember that it impacted me emotionally during my childhood and adolescence, but after going to therapy I could identify that the aftermath of divorce that "never affected me" marked my life significantly. I developed my parents' patterns, and I have unconsciously repeated their story. In my partner, I chose the parents that I refused to recognize; he was the reflection of them. I revived the same story of my parents with him. I ended the relationship and today I suffer in the flesh, with guilt, despair and the feeling of having failed my child by giving him a future similar to what I lived.

I never felt that the separation of my parents would have marked my life. I always said it was something "good" and "was the best thing for everyone", but with my behavior and my own story, I understand that my perspective on life, family and relationships was negatively impacted by the divorce of my parents and what I considered was the rupture of the outline of family that I have idealized throughout my life. ◯

Mason

I was lucky with the divorce of my parents in many ways. They divorced when I was 5, which was beneficial because I was young enough to not understand its effect. Also, my parents have remained very close throughout my childhood. I still have to answer to both parents and step-parents. The love and support I received was not hindered by the divorce, and I believe it has increased!

I have always been autonomous with the decisions I make in my life and have never let the divorce define me or hinder the decisions I make whether it be about my future plans or relationships. I worry that the divorce rate is so high, however I have to try it out for myself when the opportunity presents itself.

Vanessa

My parents' divorce happened before I was born, so I believed that their separation didn't affect me directly. The fact that I have only seen a one parent role model, —which is my mother with no presence of a father at home—might have influenced my upbringing and education.

But honestly, I think it was the best that happened in my family and to me because there has been a lot of peace and tranquility at home. My father's temperament was very difficult and my mother was not completely happy. By the way, my father died four years ago.

I want to have a family of my own where my children have the guidance of a father, but my hopes for a long term marriage are not the same, due to my parents' divorce. It makes me realize that love is not always "forever", and that couples can finish without taking into consideration their children.

Annah

I was about 13 when I discovered the reason for my parents' split, and 15 when the divorce process was finalized. It was difficult for me to see what I had considered a stable relationship and marriage fall apart. There were things that I wasn't made aware of, internal problems that, while I was playing away in my ignorant bliss, were starting to creep to the surface of my mother and father's relationship. It was especially difficult to see two people that I counted on and loved so dearly hurt and leave our family. It was the hardest for me to see my mother so torn and smashed with the knowledge of an affair, something that we had never expected to happen. The emotions were thick and heartbreaking.

Due to this, my relationships have always had a constant presence of anxiety, stress, and lack of trust. Despite my mother's awareness and concern for mine and my brother's well-being, this nurturing still hasn't prevented me from being impacted greatly by the lack of respect from the other party. Due to this, I believe that I will never be able to marry and that I will never be able to find a love that is strong enough for me to throw aside my insecurities and hesitation to trust someone fully and completely. I will always and forever be on my guard.

But, for the time being, marriage is the lowest priority, something that I have learned is not the most important thing. This has developed from my feminism and through my personal experiences with what marriage is considered to be.

Ericka

The separation of my parents was an event that didn't cause too much suffering since it happened when I was very little. My father took me with him and I still live with him. Even though it is tough not to have both parents, and in moments I wish I had my mother with me, I have a good relationship with both of them and I feel perfectly fine with that.

I still have a positive attitude with regards to marriage, so much that I am engaged to my boyfriend and our plan is to get married. I think not everybody has the same luck, so whatever has happened to your parents it doesn't mean that it will happen to you.

Lexi

Being a child of divorce forces you to endure a different kind of pain. It causes you to ask yourself what is true. It creates doubts, uncertainty and insecurity. I think it breaks you down in many ways, but like any trial or tribulation, it provides an opportunity for growth. From the rubble of a broken home can come a child who has transformed into a stronger, more insightful individual.

For many years I spent my energy focusing on the terrible things I had gone through and the wrecking ball that had devastated my family life, until I realized that I was the one choosing to feel this way. It took me many years to forgive my dad for walking out on us, but now I can honestly say I am thankful. I am thankful for many reasons, first because I am happy to say that my mother is now married to a wonderful man. Second, because it provided me with the insight that I can use to help others who are suffering. Lastly, because I learned the hard way about what love truly means and how to identify all other attributes I do not want in a lifelong partnership.

I know now that love, marriage, is a choice and not just a warm fuzzy feeling that stays between people "because they are meant to be". Marriage is hard, but I believe it should be forever. If I ever do get married I know how not to go about things, and I think that is a good place to start.

Bijan

Since my parents' divorce, I have spent countless occasions comparing my family life to that of others. I'm constantly trying to situate my family experience on a spectrum that runs from "dysfunctional" to "concrete." I'm placing others on that spectrum as well—and it's obstructing the natural progression of socialization. When contemplating relationships, or attempting to build on them, this problem intensifies.

Divorce has caused me to dwell on the past and worry about the future. I've wasted so much time and opportunities in my recent life. Giving up that mentality can be very difficult. Divorce brings depression, yes—but what is worse is the stagnation that poisons your being. You lose faith in yourself and become content with your "broken family" situation. You accept it, and do so in a pessimistic and bitter manner.

I feel lucky that the raw impacts of divorce came into my life at a later time. I can't imagine having to struggle with such a deeply personal experience as a child. It has strengthened me as an adult, but probably would've broken me as a kid.

Jessica

The day my parents told me that they were separating I was happy to know it was the end of a difficult chapter and the best decision my parents could have made for my future. All I could think was "oh yes that means my father can no longer harm my mother. " Though this change of life's path was difficult, at times I saw a power in my mother that I did not know one person could possess.

As a teenager I felt resentment for my father but now understand that he had a mental illness and his self-treatment was toxic. I find myself observing relationships that I perceive as healthy and making mental notes of how to love a partner. I have learned what not to seek; now I'm trying to figure out what to seek in a future partner. My responsibilities of education and financial security are imperative to secure prior to any concrete discussions about children. ◯

Maria

When posed with the question, how did your parents' divorce impact your life? It is very hard to come up with an answer! My parents were married, or better said stuck in a bad marriage, for 30 years. It was only last year that they decided to split ways and lead separate lives, and I can state without hesitation that both their divorce and dysfunctional relationship has impacted my life immensely. It has changed the way I live and love. The divorce process has been a time of profound sadness and despair... it is so hard to see two people you love so dearly tear each other apart in court. It's heartbreaking to see the individuals who tucked you in at night when you were a little girl not even say hello to each other if they suddenly coincide at a given place and time.

When it comes to me I can say that I'm the sort of person who has a hard time relating to others. It is really hard for me to connect with people and establish meaningful and long lasting relationships. This is especially true when it comes to a relationship with a significant other! I am 26 years old and I have never been in a serious, committed long-term relationship. I have a profound fear of relationships. The very thought of being in a serious relationship paralyzes me beyond belief. I'm terrified of repeating my parents' mistakes, of following in their footsteps, of having what they had. So I put up a wall, where I did not allow others to see me or get to know the real me. Moreover at times I feel that I am not worthy of love and connection. However, lately I feel lonely and I yearn for connection, love and belonging. Now I'm trying to tear down that wall, heal my wounds and open my heart to a new chapter in my life. I am allowing myself to be seen, deeply seen. I am now starting to ask the universe for that thing that I deprived myself from due to fear, shame and guilt. I'm honestly and openly asking the universe and God for a partner, someone to love, respect and share my life with. Hopefully someone to do things differently with and not repeat my parents' mistakes!

Ingrid

My parents' divorce was pretty heartbreaking for a 12 year old, and it came as a complete shock. After a couple of weeks of serious sadness, I tried taking on the role as the family mediator, but ended up as the family punching bag. My parents and my sister fought more than ever, my sister took out most of her anger on me, while at the same time I tried to counsel my father as he mourned our broken family. I felt ignored by both my parents as they were focusing on my increasingly rebellious sister.

Stemming from a divorced family like that has made me realize how important it is not to lose sight of yourself even if the people closest to you are in a whirlwind of chaos. I would take on everyone else's problems and this prevented me from having my own life experiences. For example, as a protective mechanism, I've always tried to make sure to be the "dumper" instead of the "dumpee," perhaps in a subconscious effort to avoid how crushed I saw my dad felt when my mother left him.

Despite this, I am for the first time in a healthy relationship where I've tried to let go of past anxieties so I can trust in my own independent instincts and hopefully overcome any trust issues I have from the divorce. ○

Jon

I was pretty lucky with my situation. My brother and I were around 8-10 years old, and our parents were able to remain good friends after they split up. My mom was struggling with her idea that she was a lesbian, and when she knew she was, they got divorced. It affected my brother at the time a little more than it did me, but the situation to us quickly became water under the bridge because of our parents' great relationship with one another.

Megan

Divorce—could not wait for it to be over. Their marriage had turned very ugly to the point of violence; but the divorce brought out greed and selfishness. I wonder if married couples in the process of divorce think about the kids.

From my experience with divorce, there are a few things I have decided. The word love comes in many forms and must be continuously worked for. I can tell someone I love them only when I know it to be true, never before. Living through my parents' divorce also has taught me that if I am in a divorce situation, I must talk with my children, ask for their opinions and be careful about what I share and say in front of them.

Anna

My parents' divorce was a long time coming. I think I always knew that they would split up. The divorce was the best thing that ever happened to me in my life at the time. I remember the relief it brought and celebrating with my mother and sister.

My parents' relationship has affected me both positively and negatively. In the end it is more positive than negative. It represents my mother's triumph in leaving an abusive husband and her ability to finally do right by my sister and me. This has affected my relationships positively and negatively. I would never have learned from my parents' mistakes and reversed the cycle of abuse on my father's side of the family or met my boyfriend, with whom I have an excellent relationship, if it weren't for the divorce.

All of the negative effects of my parents' relationship is due to them staying together for so long. The divorce was my real family's salvation. My real family being complete and whole without my father.

Ligia

My parents divorced when I was seven years old. I can say that it changed my life. I went through years of sadness because I didn't understand the situation they were living in, which was unsustainable. I can't say the precise moment in which I understood my parents' motives. The only thing I remember is watching my father pick up his clothes little by little, and that feeling of abyss that lasted for a few years. But now that my feelings have matured, I can say that it was the best that could happen. I learned to love them individually and not as a marriage.

All movies and stories are lies; happy endings for a human being are much more than just marry the person you love. Marriage is just the beginning of a new life of two people. The divorce of my parents affected my perception of happiness and my beliefs regarding the institution of marriage. All my other feelings regarding plans in my life and relationships continue to be the same.

Cherish

My parents divorced when I was 6 months old; they were together for 6 years—it makes me smile to know they once loved each other. I never cried over their break up because both of them were in my life and as far as I knew, their parenting wasn't affected by their personal relationship. Both of my parents remarried and had 2 more children each. I often felt I was in the middle and had to referee between the two and as a result, I grew up pretty fast.

This has affected my outlook on relationships. A few weeks ago, I broke up with my boyfriend of 5 years—I'm not ready for the married life and kids.

I believe children shouldn't have to be witness to their parents' dysfunctional relationships; it takes away their innocence.

Nick

I was five when my parents got divorced so it's really the only life that I know or remember. I split time equally between my parents' houses first alternating weekly, then bi-weekly as I got older. Not only did I grow up in two different households, but those two households were also evolving in ways that the traditional nuclear family does not. With step-parents, half-siblings, extended step-families, etc.—family means something much more fluid to me than to most.

If there is one thing divorce taught me at a very young age, it's that there is always more than one way to do something and there are two angles in any situation—if not more. For many people dealing with change and differing views, values, and beliefs is a challenge or a struggle, but for me it's one of the best parts about life and I think the main reason for that is my experience with divorce.

I think one of the major keys was our dad's insistence that we are not victims. I think that a lot of people feel like victims of divorce, but that's not a belief I subscribe to.

Hannah

When my best friend's parents split in the 5th grade, I was heartbroken over how hard it was on her and her sisters. My parents promised me I had no need to worry because they were "those parents" that would be together forever. When they split up 6 years later, after 20 years of marriage, it was almost a relief. Knowing how unhappy my parents were together allowed the split to make sense to me, and I felt that it would be better in the end.

Finding out later that week about the affair changed everything. I didn't speak to my dad for many months, and to this day I have not yet fully reestablished that relationship. Unfortunately, my dad didn't realize that he was cheating on my sisters and me too. I have never felt more betrayed in my life. My dad's actions have made me a much more cautious person, and I have a harder time fully trusting men in my life.

The biggest effect my parents' divorce has had on me is my dislike in planning ahead in my relationships. The expectation of being happy in the future, as a family, was crushed for me, so I'm scared to make those plans for myself and have another person destroy them for me. ○

Cloe

The separation of my parents happened when I was a baby, and since then I have lived with my father's family. During my childhood I suffered a lot because I didn't understand what had happened. I always asked myself: Why did my mom leave me? Why did they get separated? But through time I could understand better—thanks to my father's family. I feel very fortunate to grow up with them since they provided me with what my parents didn't.

Until now my perception about marriage has not affected my goals. I have understood that my parent's mistakes don't have to determine my future; on the contrary, I wish to have a stable family and that my children don't go through what I went through.

Samantha

My parents were married for 10 years and them getting divorced was like getting hit by a ton of bricks. I was about 15; my father was cheating on my mother. It's made the relationship with my father miserable. I want, for many reasons, to forgive him but I just can't find it within myself to do so. What's the worst is that when you are the only one of your friends going through this, you feel alone. You are trapped inside your own head with your own thoughts with only yourself to give you answers. I alienated myself from everyone except my brothers; their coping methods were as bad as mine.

The divorce twisted and warped my trust in my relationships. Now I am in a relationship, where I can't be fully open with or trust the person I am with because I think to myself that it's only a matter of time before he will leave me, like my father had done to my mother. He has never given me reason to ever think he would do something like that, but I always think if my father could be with my mother, the woman he called his soul mate, and cheat on her, that is enough for me to believe that anyone I will ever be with can and will do the same thing to me.

My trust has gotten better as the years have gone on, but the thought of being betrayed is still a constant gnawing at the back of my brain.

Tony

My parents divorced my sophomore year of high school after it became apparent that my mother was an alcoholic and my father was codependent and emotionally, sometimes physically, abusive. The main thing I remember about that period was a sense of terror in the uncertainty: was dad in jail? Did mom drink her way back into the hospital? But I also remember feeling constantly defiant—not just of them, but of everything that was out of my control. I thought things like "They don't deserve kids like me and Mary" or "Maybe if I screamed louder, tried harder…"

I do talk to my parents now—not dad so much because I blame him for me having to live in a homeless shelter for a month and being sexually assaulted while I was there. My parents' divorce made me feel more alone than I'd ever felt before. It even separated me from Mary, my sister, who I consider to be the heart and soul behind everything that I do. She now lives with my aunt and uncle (who don't approve of me and I do not get along with) so I can't see her. I'll never forgive my parents for pulling us apart.

Comments

At first glimpse, Karen Klein's photographs in *Broken Circle* transcribe a buoyancy and freshness that is inescapably tied to youth. But you must read closely to get their full impact. Klein's photographs offer the rare, even impolite, pleasure of a lingering gaze. As you look into these candid faces remember that photographs disguise more than they reveal. There are shadows and specters here. Klein has done us all–divorced and united, old and young, male and female–a great service by looking closely at these wise, insistent faces and recording their voices giving form to previously uncaptured thoughts. The words and the portraits amplify each other; they are interdependent texts, just as children are with their parents (and vice versa).

–George Slade - Photography Curator, Consultant, and Writer

I have practiced family law for over 30 years and handled countless, often high-conflict, custody cases. I have also been divorced and raised three sons. Many professionals in the law and mental health communities, as well as professional organizations, have tried to find the means to communicate to parents how devastating divorce can be to the health and welfare of children. Yet the programs and materials often come across as preachy and difficult to access. The importance of Karen Klein's *Broken Circle* project is that it simply and effectively conveys the consequences children often experience.

–Nancy Zalusky Berg - Walling Berg & Debele, President, United States Chapter, International Academy of Matrimonial Lawyers

As a psychiatrist who has worked exclusively with college students for nearly two decades, I am familiar with the high numbers of those who share histories of parental divorce as well as the impact of divorce on their emotions, self confidence, and intimate relationships. These are often secret histories, perhaps alluded to when inquired about, but rarely expanded upon within their usual support network. Even in the confidential confines of therapy it may take some time before these young adults are comfortable in confronting and expressing their feelings which often include a sense of abandonment, shame, confusion, anger, and/or lack of trust. Art provides a therapeutic venue that is often overlooked. By coupling autobiographical prose with photographic expressions, Karen Klein's *Broken Circle* project unveils the lasting influence of parental divorce on the lives of young men and women. Often tragic, occasionally welcomed, it is evident that divorce continues to cast a shadow over the foundation of trust essential for current and future relationships. Yet one detects a sense of relief, even healing, in these youthful adults, enabled by the self-expression that only portrait photography and the written word can reveal. It is evident that this has been a therapeutic journey for these men and women. Their bold declarations will undoubtedly serve as a call to others to face the challenging history of a family divorce.

–Gary Christenson, MD - Chief Medical Officer, Boynton Health Services, U of MN, and President, Global Alliance for Arts & Health

Kudos to Karen and the young adults she photographed and interviewed. The photos are a story all by themselves. The stories from the young people tell us that we are much too casual about the "resilience of children" to parental conflict. All parents need to read this book, as there is conflict in intact as well as divorcing families. If parents listen to these young people and work at developing healthy parent-child relationships, everybody wins.

−Mary Davidson - Retired Hennepin County District Court Judge

The experience of divorce for children is heart wrenching, no matter what the circumstances, and Karen Klein's *Broken Circle* project poignantly portrays that experience. The Buddhists say there are only a few times in each of our lives that we experience our own "world collapse" and obviously, when viewing the photographs and reading the commentaries from the participants, for many of them, this is one of those times. I can only hope for all children experiencing the disorientation of divorce, that standing on the shoulders of your parents, learning from parents' mistakes, going beyond where your parents have gone, working very hard at becoming, yourself, a trustworthy person is the gold that can be mined from these very difficult circumstances.

−Carol Wichers, MA, LICSW, LMFT - Family Counseling

As a therapist and researcher, I have heard and read many personal stories of children of divorce, but I have never seen this kind of powerful juxtaposition of gripping words and haunting photography. Karen Klein allowed these young adults to express themselves in their own terms, unencumbered by what their elders might impose on them. The photographs and personal statements are marked by clarity and ambivalence, subtlety and simplicity, vulnerability and resilience. We don't give young people a place to express themselves about the long shadow that divorce casts on their lives, especially divorce not handled well by the parents. The *Broken Circle* project opens up that opportunity and enriches us all.

−William J. Doherty, Ph.D. - Professor of Family Social Science, and Director of the Minnesota Couples on the
 Brink Project, U of MN

Broken Circle offers a powerful, visual testament to how young people navigate the complex emotional seas of divorce. Each of these images looks directly into us, while the accompanying text offers honest responses to conversations and questions ordinarily avoided. And along with the expected feelings of loss and mistrust, there are some hopeful surprises—relief, hope, connection, and a strength that can only come from moving through and transcending adversity.

−Glenn Hirsch, Ph.D. - Licensed Psychologist, Director of Counseling & Consulting Services, U of MN

Comments (cont.)

As a divorce mediator and former Family Court Judicial Officer, I have always emphasized that the actions of parents toward their children in a divorce have lasting impacts long beyond the age of 18 when the Court's jurisdiction ends. Karen Klein's *Broken Circle* project encapsulates the impact of divorce on young adults by empowering the children to speak from their souls, often in heart-wrenching terms. The stories of the young adults are brought to life through Karen's powerful photographs, which allow the reader a rare glimpse into the source of the profound narrative that weaves through her book.

−Kevin McGrath - Family Law Mediator, McGrath Dispute Resolution, LLC

It is so important for children to have a voice when families divorce. With support, a safe place to ask questions and to honor their emotions, children can successfully transition from a one-home to a two-home family even when their parents struggle. Karen's project offers these youth a special opportunity to express themselves and continue their search for understanding.

−Patricia Rogers - Licensed Clinical Social Worker, Collaborative Divorce Coach and Neutral Child Specialist

As a psychologist, parenting coach, and divorce mediator, I am often asked how parents can hear the voices of their children during times of separation and divorce. Karen Klein has provided a collective voice of children of divorce in her *Broken Circle* project. The direct gaze of the young adults in these photographs and their un-edited words provide a powerful view into their complex perspectives, battle scars, and the wisdom gained from their experiences of parental divorce. May their words guide those who are separating to find the strength and compassion to navigate their children through rough waters, so the children may emerge, not lost and grieving, but changed and strengthened by having been helped to successfully navigate their family's adversity.

−Kirsten Lysne, Ph.D., - Licensed Psychologist, Moxie Inc.

The *Broken Circle* project confronts us with the faces and voices of divorce in a way that has a deep and lasting impact. Each page provides a wakeup call that makes it impossible to ignore the true impact of divorce. For those of us who work with divorcing families, this book serves as a constant and powerful reminder on how children experience the divorce of their parent. Every divorce professional should have a copy available in their waiting rooms, offices and conference rooms so that we can sense the real presence of children during these important times.

−Ron Ousky - Collaborative Attorney and Mediator, co-author of The Collaborative Way to Divorce.

The *Broken Circle* project provides a unique look at the long term effects of divorce on children. The power of each parent's individual decisions during divorce is made evident by the scars shown through the words and images captured by Karen. The simplicity of the *Broken Circle* project is what makes its impact so dramatic; there is no need for fancy interpretations or implied messaging. These grown-up children of divorce provide a poignant and honest understanding of the long-term implications of divorce.

−Jai Kissoon - Chief Executive Officer, the OurFamilyWizard® website

Can a divorce process be a healing process? It definitely needs to be if we learn anything from the voices and faces of the young adults depicted in Karen Klein's *Broken Circle* project. A divorce process that supports the parents, gives children a voice, and is focused on the needs and interests of all family members can make all the difference in a child's experience of their parents' divorce.

−Tonda Mattie - Collaborative Family Law Attorney, Past President of the Collaborative Law Institute (CLI)

Most of what we know about the complex and often long-lasting effects of divorce comes from social scientists who have conducted research on − not with − adult children whose lives have been (and continue to be) so impacted by the decisions that their parents have made. The Broken Circle Project is an extraordinary departure from this. Instead of impersonal statistics, facts, or figures, we are hearing these young people's stories through their own voices and words. We are seeing their pain and vulnerability, alongside their strength and resiliency, in their faces and in their eyes. This project offers something that no academic text or therapist could offer.

−Tai J. Mendenhall, Ph.D., LMFT - Assistant Professor of Family Social Science and Associate Director of the Citizen Professional Center, University of Minnesota

Not surprisingly, many of the stories have raw and painful edges. Divorce is extremely difficult for children. The young adults in the *Broken Circle* project who experienced feelings of abandonment and loss, or those for whom parental conflict was high or remains active, are still struggling to find equilibrium and a sense of emotional security. Many participants acknowledged to Karen that this was the first time they could remember having the opportunity to talk about how they felt about the divorce. Their participation in the project was cathartic and healing. However, what is hopeful is that not all the stories were negative or bleak. The young adults whose parents had divorced in a respectful or amicable way, and those whose parents were on friendly terms as co-parents tended to express acceptance, balance and hope for the future.

−Deborah Clemmensen - M.Eq., Licensed Psychologist, Neutral Child Specialist in Collaborative Law

Karen Klein is a photographer/visual artist currently living in Sarasota, Florida. She holds an MFA degree in studio arts from the University of Minnesota, where, in 1987, she undertook the photography project that would more than two decades later lead to *Broken Circle—Children of Divorce and Separation*.

After working in the corporate environment until 2007, Klein returned to her art fulltime. Over the years, she evolved her signature approach: long-term projects exploring personal issues of universal import, often including collaboration. In these she may use film and/or digital, color and/or black and white, and varied stylistic approaches—from the portraiture of *Broken Circle—Children of Divorce and Separation*, the complex, multi-layered collage of *In Focus, Out of Memory* and *Random Works* to the new body of work, *Something Almost Being Said*. Klein's photography invites the viewer in artistically as well as thematically, often alluding to social concerns.

Karen Klein's photographs are in many private and public collections.

www.brokencircleproject.org
www.karenklein.com

For more information regarding acquisition or exhibition opportunities or to become a participant please email: karen@karenklein.com

Made in the USA
Lexington, KY
14 March 2019